To
Carl

Warmest regards
Bernadette Bland

May 8, 2014

Flights of Fancy

A Book of Poetry, Prose, and Imaginative Short Stories

Bernadette Bland

iUniverse, Inc.
Bloomington

Flights of Fancy
A Book of Poetry, Prose, and Imaginative Short Stories

iUniverse books may be ordered through booksellers or by contacting:

iUniverse
1663 Liberty Drive
Bloomington, IN 47403
www.iuniverse.com
1-800-Authors (1-800-288-4677)

ISBN: 978-1-4502-8452-3 (pbk)
ISBN: 978-1-4502-8453-0 (ebk)

Printed in the United States of America

iUniverse rev. date: 2/17/2011

"No matter the attitude, mood, or circumstance, keep on dreaming. Do not be deterred from your heart's desire."
—Bernadette Bland

For my parents,
James P. and A. Jessie (Hughes) Smith,
and my sister, Miriam Whewell,
for all their love and encouragement to write
and my son Patrick for his renderings of the
young Indian Warrior and the eagle.

Contents

Introduction

Flights of Fancy is a book of poetry in which I tried to express the imagery, beauty, and emotional rollercoaster we all experience in this world of which we are such an integral part. I hope to share this rhythmical creation with readers everywhere.

Drifting Grace: God's Art Show

The delicate bits of crystal lace,
Feel them tickle as they kiss your face.
Playful and lively, yet with artful grace;
All nestle together and settle in place.

Slouching in valleys,
Adorning high peaks,
Tucking close the stone walls,
And frosting wooded creeks.

Laying low the tree boughs
And flattening tall grass;
It makes caps for the rocks
and ornaments window glass.

The snow drifts, and blows,
and makes cold your nose,
which gives forth a rosy show
Like an ember's glow.

These crystals are a sight,
So pristine and white;
Dancing on breezes, so feathery light.
Reflecting the silvery moon up on high,
O' so bright in their dazzling night flight.

More beautiful sights shall never be,
Than this graceful wintry portrait
That is painted by God for you and for me.

The Sea

Caught up in its omnipotence,
the Sea can consume you.
It can fill you with rapture … or
It can steal your life!

Yet, on its gently lapping shores,
Its hushed whispers soothe contentedly,
Its fragrance transcending.

Inspirational for far-off dreams
And illusory planes,
Its perpetual motion instills
an unfathomable peace
And a oneness
with the power and nature of God!

Sound Reflections

The Beauty of Sound...

in the thrilling strings of the violin virtuoso Itzhak Perlman, the gloried fullness of a symphony orchestra; the silvered tenor notes of Josh Groban or Placido Domingo; the pureness and clarity of tone found only in the mellow notes of a wooden native flute; the infectious delight of a baby's laughter; the beautiful vocals of Barbara Streisand; the intensity of feeling in the unique music and words of Garth Brooks ... these are what set the imagination free to create a vision of one's own. The distinctiveness of their sounds inspires beyond the visual senses.

If there is ever to be one sense I must lose, I pray it not be my sense of hearing—a world of beauty one can ill afford to lose.

Mama

Through the eyes of memory I can see her there,
In a crown of tawny gold and skin so fair:
Seated by the window, brushing long hair,
Watching us kids from her rocking chair.

Then there was gray in that crown so fine,
and delicate lines, now added with time.
On and on she strove, seeming never to tire,
Filled with energy untold like a blazing spitfire.
The gray turned to spun silver, her step slowed with age;
The fair skin's still a wonder, its texture unfazed.

Then one day she lay quiet, her spirit ever gone.
She was my sparkle in life, now my grief to mourn.

The locket she gave, my heart's dearest treasure,
A thought from her to cherish forever.
To this very day her vivid memory lives, her loving within me,
Was her gift to give.

Dedicated to my beloved mother.

Memories

Snuggled on his lap,
Held close in his arms,
He sang me sweet songs
Of "Endearing Young Charms."

Safe and cozy for me,
My own world to be;
Cuddled near to his heart,
From which I ne'er wanted
to part.

From him, all around
Love did abound;
From his heart, his eyes,
His lips, and his mind.

A tender touch, laughing ways,
A crooked smile, and caring days;
Reaping memories of poems,
Stories, and songs … for all of my days.

For this *daddy* of mine
forever will be a living image
In my memory.

Forever Cherished

Cherished are we and the times we spent,
Doing nothing in particular, going to no special event.
Travelin' the road with kids in tow,
A bag of fifteen-cent hamburgers, and off we'd go.

Special times … for just us two,
Doing whatever we wanted to do.
The beach, a drive, dinner on the pier,
Spontaneous moments held, oh, so dear.

These treasured memories keep love close;
The intervening years have naught to boast.
Impulsiveness and laughter, our time was free;
Forever Cherished will be this sweet memory.

Wind Speak

The wind speaks in whispers while rustling playfully through a field of brilliant wildflowers.

In banshee wails … chilling and shivery
On dark stormy nights.

With icy shrieks forecasting the bitterest cold
Of a frigid nor'easter.

In gentle teasing laughter
On a bright day in spring.

Or in breathy, sensuous air drafts
That waft the scent of sweet roses.

With gusty howls of danger
When nature goes array.

In mellowed accents of cool breezes
From ocean currents;
Over dewy country farmlands,
In mountain high meadows;
Over rivers and deserts,
And through wastelands, grasslands, and swamplands.

The wind speaks of all of these,
As only it can.
Listen to it … breathe it in,
And you will know of its eloquence.

God's Handwriting

The stillness of the crystalline dawn
Slips gently into day,
Scattering star bright effervescence
In a serene and godlike way.

The shimmering, frosty landscape
Captures tranquil beauty unrivaled;
A glistening desert land of drifted crystal sand,
Written in God's own Majestic hand.

An artisan bold, He sculpts and He chisels.
New fantasies He designs out of crusty ice drizzle;
A mercurial visage, an ever-transient mirage.

Then, at day's end,
By the radiant glow of the high-risen moon,
The diamond oasis sparkles;
It reflects in exquisite wonder, a pristine lace comforter.

Adorned in prism-like crystals,
Such beauteous artistry can only be
The handwriting of God, Creator of all that you see!

Princess Maddy Grace

She has hair of burnished gold
and skin of cream…
soulful, dark eyes.
She is a dream—
Princess Maddy Grace.

She's young and bright,
having nary a fright,
with a warm and friendly personality—
and she is only three,
Princess Maddy Grace.

No one can be above her;
To know her is to love her.
For she will always be
My beautiful granddaughter,
And she is very special to me,
Princess Maddy Grace.

Princess Maddy Grace and her trusty steed, Daisy

I'll Huff and I'll Puff

A creature of infinite variation, the wind is one minute blustery; pushing people around with gusto; knocking over objects in his great zeal to show off his prowess; stealing hats and sometimes getting frisky with the ladies' skirts, causing them dismal embarrassment. Next, he plays cute and coquettish. He is as enchanting and amorous as any lover, rustling your hair and stroking your body with whisper-soft caresses; and sensuous though it may seem, it is but a façade. It is his greatest joke—to pacify and catch you off guard.

So, be forewarned. This blowsy fellow is more fickle than the blackest-hearted villain and can regress to spitefulness in the blink of an eye. Capable of turning a hundred and eighty out, he can become suddenly brisk—frigid even—freezing one out of his good graces!

He storms about in a foul temper, howling lustily in a demonic wail and profiling a macho display of undeniable and triumphant power. He sometimes lets his temper run riot, destroying all in his path, just to vent his senseless anger.

Finally, exhausted and mollified, he whistles quite a different tune. He breezes merrily about the woodland, making the trees bow and shiver in ecstasy to his lilting song. With great zeal, he tugs playfully at the clinging leaves that grasp precariously to their lifeline but soon find themselves giving in to his high-pressure tactics. He has them dancing and spinning in haphazard abandonment, thrilling to the wild rollercoaster course he navigates for them. They ride his currents as though rafting the raging rapids of a wild and endless river.

When least expected, our crafty friend is incredibly gentle; rippling mighty oceans ever so carefully, like grandma folding cream into her pudding and smoothly blending the ingredients for the finish.

The wind is all of these things and more. He can be a consummate friend or a mortal enemy, but, like him or not, he is a part of nature and here to stay. So, whenever you hear he's comin' a blowin' your way … *Hang on to your hat* and *run for cover*!

God's Glory

The breeze's gentle caress washes me with a whisper of sweet breath, playfully teasing as it grazes by greeting the day. As I ramble along the sparsely traveled path this gorgeous spring morning, endless wonders are revealed to me. A tranquil stillness such as I have never before experienced ... heady fragrances of dewy flora ... pine musk ... rich, mossy earth ... and sweet grasses embrace me.

I am awed by the distant, shimmering mountains that undulate to a silent, sensual tempo in the misty vestiges of lingering dawn shadows ... not quite ready to acquiesce to the rising golden glory. Trilling birds create harmonious magic which rejuvenates my spirit and sends it soaring through blue heavens just peeking out from under night's dark shade, and the lowing of contented cattle echoes throughout the valley in the dawning of this new day!

God's glory? Who could deny it?!

Behind the Mask

The masked face
of the clown. Does he
laugh or frown? Behind
his bright smile, is his mood
up or
down?

His performance so
jolly, the children clap
in glee. He seems a free
soul, but how do we know?

If he cries, he weeps
inside where no one knows
he has pain to hide. But, if you see
clear, you may find a tear;
for within his heart, he is like
all of us here.

Intrusions: Seeking Solace

Salty waves sob upon the frigid shores—
Their perpetual motion a torrential plow in the
Eroding sands and passage of time.
My wounded soul is as denuded as these!

Such is the torturous rage within my heart
And the surging pain of hatred that engulfs me.
When unbidden, the memories come crashing in
Upon the frozen pebbles of my mind.

Overwhelming, drowning, and dragging at me with
Desperate, grasping claws…
Then ebbing away…
To settle once more between the ragged edges of raw,
Torn emotion.

Pals

My friend and I share a great many things. In particular, we have lots of fun sharing secrets of the exciting, and oftentimes, bewildering events of our days, usually after all has quieted down for the night within the household.

Some secrets seem big and important, while others are small, insignificant items. But as her friend and trusted keeper of secrets, I hold them safely within, never to be revealed to anyone.

My friend is a twelve-year-old girl with raven hair that flows in waves over tawny cream shoulders. Dark brows and thick black lashes adorn a smiling face of deep-set eyes that flash with golden flecks. Her overall beauty is striking, and I am in awe that she chose me to be her secret pal. We've been together for the last three years and have shared the best and worst of times.

As for me, I am rather small of stature and demure, keeping mostly to myself. Though I dread being seen out in the open, I have been considered by those who have had the occasion to catch a glimpse of me as pretty. Being quite pale, in direct contrast to my friend, my peachy pink blends make me not so unpleasant to look upon, and I am noted for my reliability as a confidant.

In spite of how pretty I may look, I try to be inconspicuous and especially hard to find (with my friend's help of course), avoiding those who would seek me out for the secrets I hold. I guess that's why I'm always the one hiding in our games of hide and seek.

My friend alone holds the key to my inner secrets, and she shares hers with me. She is my true and trusted friend, and I … I am her Diary!

Ancestry

With purity of tone do the lamented notes of the native flute

Rise and sing across the vast Southwest plains...

And the hearts of its people mourn.

The blue shadowed canyons echo the sound,
    And the soulful music abounds.

There is chanting and ritual dancing,
And the warning voices of the drums.

As the Chiefs sit in council, the
Gathering warriors prepare for the fight.
This night they celebrate ... for tomorrow they will die!
All because of different skin color,
Misunderstood cultures, and senseless hate!

"I cannot think that we are useless, or God would not have created us. There is one God, looking down on us all. We are all the children of one God. The sun; the darkness; the winds, are all listening to what we have to say."
—Geronimo

Spirits Rising

Our Spirit is free … free as the majestic eagle in flight;
Yet counsels within bitter pain great as the grizzly.
We are of the Earth … We are the People.

Less than nothing in the White Eyes world,
We have been trampled upon and slaughtered as sheep,
Lied to and torn from our very existence!
And they ask, "Why so angry?"

From wide-open plains where once we lived free,
We were herded on to patches of parched and lifeless land.
Once fiercely proud, we became a defeated people;
Demoralized and broken, our pride stripped from us,
Much the same as the lands we once roamed.

But here, in this present time,
Our spirits soar still,
Free as that mighty eagle sailing the winds of forever—
For *these spirits* will never be trapped on a reservation,
Humiliated and pained beyond endurance.

Rejuvenation: A Point of View from an Old House

I am old and tired. My walls are thin, cracked, and drafty, and my roof leaks. I have windows that are missing or smashed, and my porch has sagged right to the ground, losing its grip altogether.

I have stood here for 150 years and was once proud and strong with a spiffy white coat and a slate cap. I sported three chimneys and several fireplaces that kept me warm inside and harbored cheer for those who sheltered within my embracing frame. Luscious smells of fresh baked breads and sumptuous feasts simmering on the old wood cook stove wafted from my kitchen. Mesmerizing odors from the canning of fruits and vegetables and baked apples blended with the clean smells of soap and creamy furniture polishes; perfume to my senses.

Once upon a time, I had been surrounded by rich farmland with companion barns and sheds which housed horses and other animals, as well as implements for working the land. My caretakers produced grains and vegetables which they sold at market to maintain themselves and me. Aah ... life was good.

I was filled to the rafters with music, laughter, and soft harmonious voices. Little people abounded everywhere as they raced up and down my staircases and in and out through my many doorways. The larger folk seemed content just to be there. I was loved and well cared for.

Over the years, little by little, the changing of the guard brought about neglect and gradual deterioration; until at long last, I was abandoned altogether. Year after year, I sat, depressed and alone, uncared for and empty. Eventually, I was acquired by another for a few measly dollars and hope reared its foolish head, but the new owner didn't care for me. I was just an investment; not necessarily me, myself, but the land I sat upon.

One day, some new people came, staring at and pondering my sorry state. They won't last, I told myself; certain that once they'd left they wouldn't come back, and I'd never see them again. But, much to my amazement, a couple of days later, they showed up again, loaded down with mops, brooms, endless cleaning goods, and tons of determination. They set about stripping me of the ragged floor coverings which hid the old, but still perfectly good, wood parquet ones beneath, sweeping out the dirt and cobwebs from every corner, nook, crack, and crevice, ceiling to floor.

I sensed an uncertainty and disappointment with my current status and could almost hear them thinking: "Is all this going to be worth it?" The woman in particular was depressed with my state of affairs. I could feel her regret over my acquisition and witnessed her tears at night when all were asleep but her. I couldn't blame her. My wall spaces were crawling with all manner of creepy critters. Squirrels and chipmunks lived in my attic; not to mention the bats and other unmentionable creatures lurking in the dank darkness of my cellar. Still, they stuck with it, working slowly, but progressively, day by day, week by week I was scrubbed, dusted, vacuumed, polished, and painted. New plumbing fixtures, appliances, piping, and wiring replaced my vandalized contents, and soon my revitalized parts were chorusing new life throughout my denuded framework. Sturdy new underpinnings boosted floor joists. My strength was being renewed—and exultation was mine.

Arrival of the warmer seasons found my living room walls being stripped right to the studding, and the inside hallway was demolished to expand the area. New padding and wallboard had me warming up with new self-esteem. New paint, refurbishment of the darkly stained wood floor, and new paneled and floral dressing added to my gaiety, after which exquisite drapery and furnishings filled the emptiness. Completing that particular project, they continued on room after room, upstairs and down, giving new life wherever they touched, and I relished the ecstasy of it all.

One year, two, and suddenly, twelve years had slipped away. The roof and outside wall coverings had been retouched cosmetically, and general repairs added to the overall accomplishment, but by now, the work had been slowed and money was scarce.

Very early one morning, a group of men arrived, tools, equipment, and materials in tow; I thought I was doomed. My owners had moved out and left me in the clutches of their son. Without a moment's hesitation, they began to strip the outer coverings off my frame, baring me naked for the entire world to see. How mortifying!! But, before the evening skies turned pitch dark, they had given me a new and warmer coat to wear; and in the weeks that followed, they redressed me in a new cream-colored dress coat, replaced my roof with a cap of dark green metal with leakproof coverage, and new and stronger additions strengthened my foundations. My windows were given new glass jackets and trimming, and my chimney bricks were repointed and new flues were fitted to the insides.

I also received a special gift of softer water and better heating units in the basement and kitchen. I was given a new attachment by way of a replacement porch, for the one which had crumbled away so very long ago, a concrete pathway leading to my back door, as well as a concrete apron and steps for my new side entrance. I was brand new again … almost.

Now, several years later, I stand tall, proud, and strong once more; ready perhaps for yet another 150 years of loving families, laughing children, music, and entertainment to fill me up with blessings.

My cup runneth over!

Friendships Rare

There is nothing to compare to the loving bond they share;
Tis' true friends … not fair.

The truth of such friends touches the soul,
Comforts the heart, and gives peace to the mind.
They are gracious and kind.

Though words are not uttered, their actions speak loud;
They give forth great warmth, and render feelings so proud.
Through good times and bad, no need to explain,
A friend knows so well your joy and your pain.

Understanding and steadfast, do not pretend;
You are who you are. Be an honest, good friend,
And reach out with love; have faith in mankind.
This treasure from God is of the exceptional kind.

My Coworker Family

My family at the office here, *I hold very dear.*
We are all friends, and their kindness never ends.

The year I spent working here,
The laughter we shared and the fun we had,
Shall forever remain within my heart,
Never to be forgot.

Now separated by miles and time
apart from you all,
Your love and mindfulness
Will always be like gold.

Patty's House

Patty's house is very dear to her,
as dear as her puppies—don't you know?
She had it all redone,
which for her was not any fun;
those contractors really caused her to bum-m-m-m!

So she threw a little party
to show off her new potty,
the bright, new kitchen, and her door
with its fancy bow.

The sofa she'd been made to scrub clean of mud,
Caused by the boots of the worker who'd slept the job through,
made poor Patty turn *livid blue.*

Oh, she sighed a great big, wheew!!
When at last they were through,
she could sob boo hoo
with relief, but pain too.

And if time should require a repeat of the scene,
Patty would probably pooh pooh it.
"In your dreams, honey bunny," she'd say.

But after a laugh, or in about a year and a half,
when the torment's been long since forgotten,
the dream may reawake—and that's all it would take
to start the whole thing over again!!

Rebecca

Meticulous of taste and lovely of face—
She is clear in faith and is filled with grace,
Rebecca.

She is Rebecca.
Truth in friendship, honesty, and respect,
she transcends what we expect,
Rebecca.

A selfless caregiver and coworker too,
A young Mother as well, her son only two.
She worries and frets, yet never forgets.
She is Rebecca.

A true sense of kindness has she
and with malice toward none.
She is ... only *one*,
Rebecca.

Lovin' Folk

With open hearts you are welcomed there—
To a place of warmth, giving, and cherished care.
Their homes, their lives, their all they share
With those so fortunate, to know these extraordinaire!

The joy, the laughter, the wealth of their love
Sown abundantly and freely from the heart,
Gives enduring comfort, contentment, and peace.
It is a gift through them from above.

God's grace truly lives within each one;
His Blessed Spirit shines brilliantly forth.
Usually such goodness and unselfish love goes
Unnoticed by most and unsung.

But, Lord, let it be your destiny for me,
To remain in your presence through them.
And may the examples of their unconditional love
Be mine to give as Your gift from above.

Ok'tober Nights

A haloed silver moon is heightened
By the west's dark and cloudy light;
A wood smoke aroma is drifting
On brisk and bracing breezes,
This cool Ok'tober Night.

Feelings of déjà vu, this strange peacefulness does bring;
Of other long-ago times, and of other enchanting
Ok'tober Nights.

Christmas Is Love

A time for reaching out, Christmas is the time for loving and sharing; most especially with those in need from loneliness, looking for friendship, who are filled with bitterness and lack of faith, or are separated by great distances from beloved family and friends. The season of the Christ child is such when human hearts warm up to the joy and cheer of the season and the meaning of giving. The following is a story of that special warmth and the joy of giving ... and receiving.

Alone in a strange city, far from the small town where she'd lived since her birth, the young woman was to discover this most special kind of love; a reaching out from the heart, the best that humankind has to offer.

Uncertain and afraid, Bridget and her children fled for their lives, leaving home, family, and all that was familiar in order to seek safe shelter from the tyranny that was her husband and his mother. They left everything behind, except what few belongings could be thrown into a couple of paper sacks, and headed for a new life and, hopefully, survival. Three months in their new surroundings found Bridget working long hours as a waitress. Before school began, she'd brought the kids to work with her. The bosses, sympathetic to her situation, allowed them to stay provided they behaved appropriately. On that score she knew that there would be no problem, and they soon became the darlings of the regular patrons, who spoiled them with all kinds of goodies. Even the lady boss took to giving them "red quarters" designated for the jukebox so that they could play their favorite songs. Mr. Boss gave them special treats from the kitchen, in addition to all the soda and milk they could drink. The children also got two daily meals, which went a long way towards making the tight budget stretch just a little further. Life felt strange. Though it was a constant struggle, it was getting better. The consumptive fear that had held them so immobile for the last nine years was gradually easing, and they began to relax into this new life, at least as much as the situation allowed. Bridget, herself, felt almost exuberant with her newfound freedom. The terror that her husband would find them and make good on his threat to kill her began to fade, and life was looking brighter.

Bridget eventually learned from a trusted friend back home that she and the kids had been written off as nonexistent, and her relief was overwhelming.

No more would they have to live in fear of unfamiliar cars slowly circling the court's driveway, and gone was the gnawing fear of being suddenly confronted with a shotgun. Life could be good after all!

The approaching Christmas season brought its own depression when Bridget suddenly realized what a bleak and lonesome Christmas it would be for all of them. She missed her family terribly, and most nights found her crying well into the wee hours. This Christmas would not be like the ones they'd previously known, for there would be little to nothing for the kids in the way of presents … or a tree. Christmas dinner was likely to be nonexistent, but she was determined to make the holidays as cheery as possible. She would save every penny she could manage, and each child would have at least the one thing they wanted the most, or its closest equivalent. They would have Christmas dinner, too; maybe not turkey and all the trimmings, but it would be the best and most festive she could create. They would be happy with that; she would see to it.

Christmas Eve dawned cloudy and cold, and while getting ready for work, Bridget mused about what to get the kids with the few dollars she'd managed to save. She planned to go to the big Christmas Eve toy sale at the mall after work to see what she could find. They had never been well off financially, so the kids would be satisfied to have just one gift a piece. They were great kids and rarely, if ever, complained about their hard times. With the dinner she was planning and a bright and cheerful attitude, they would have a great Christmas, she told herself.

That evening at the end of her shift, the bosses called everyone together and presented each employee with a gift of a beautiful five pound ham and a five-dollar Christmas bonus. Through grateful tears, she left for the shopping mall, dropping off a friend in need of a ride home on the way. Arriving at his place, he invited her in to meet his girlfriend and have some hot cocoa to thank her for going out of her way to bring him home. Warmed from the cocoa, she murmured her thanks and made for the door, but not before he'd placed a large bag of fruit in her arms. "By way of thanks for the lift home," he said, and quickly added that there was a really nice turkey for five dollars at the store where he worked which he'd had set aside for her earlier. She should drop by and pick it up, he instructed, using her bonus to pay for it. With tears brimming and expressing her deep felt appreciation, she headed out for her shopping spree.

Purchases made, she headed home with a light heart. The precious turkey and the bag of fruit she unpacked, only later to discover that it also contained all the vegetables she'd need for her dinner, and on the very bottom, a five dollar bill tucked in the last of the carrots. Tears ran down her face as she thought of this act of true kindness.

Supper preparations were underway when there was a knock at the door. The mailman stood on the doorstep with a huge box, which he claimed was hers. Puzzled, she opened it and found it filled with gaily wrapped packages in a bedding of lovely new and used clothing for the children. More tears! The box was from her former sister-in-law in Florida who'd told her decidedly that leaving her mean-spirited brother had been the best thing she could have done.

Later, having put away the clothes and stacked the packages in a corner of the living room, Bridget made ready to take the kids next door so she could go shopping for the promised presents. There had been no time after work after all.

There was a knock on the door, again, and then it flew open and in trooped friends she'd recently met, part of the regular customers from the restaurant where she worked, plus her next door neighbor. They were all carrying bags of groceries, more fruit and nuts, an artificial Christmas tree with all the necessary trimmings, and a small artificial fireplace, including greens for the top. Astonishment rendered her speechless as her heart filled to near bursting. She sobbed, overwhelmed with sheer joy, and everyone else went about setting up the tree and the fireplace and decorating the room. They'd also brought along some spiked eggnog with which to celebrate the Season of Giving. The kids were totally enraptured with all that was happening.

As they were all leaving, someone mentioned that the greens on the fireplace could use some readjustment, and following through on the idea, she found tucked amongst the boughs a twenty dollar bill. Once again, the tears overflowed, her heart so filled with gratitude that she found it difficult to breathe.

Little had Bridget realized just how kind people really could be, which served to confirm her earlier conclusions. She was indelibly impressed by their unforgettable attitudes of pure joy in loving and caring and giving. The great nature of these very special friends, people who only a few short months before had been total strangers, was a beacon from God, not unlike the Star of Bethlehem over the manger at Christ's birth. It was the most awesome and enlightening Christmas she'd ever experienced; one she'd never forget for an eternity.

Reflections

I am nearest God when I am:

* Imagining myself in a flowering mountain meadow, wild and free as the wind that musses my hair and tickles my senses.

* Meditating in a great silent forest, captivated by the harmonies of Earth's nature symphony.

* Basking in the summer warmth and solitude of a secluded cove, lulled by the whisper of gentle waves nuzzling the shore.

* Intrigued by rocky shores where mournful fog horns cry out on misty nights, while churning buoys toll warning knells to fog-blinded ships and shrieking gulls SOS mariners venturing dangerously close to land fall.

* Mesmerized by the lonesome echo of a distant passing train.

* Enraptured by the melodic enchantment of the Boston Pops, or lost in the simple, soulful, flowing breath of a Native American flute.

* Delighting in life's joys and basking in the limitless love of Almighty God.

* Just trying to live as we were created to live; sharing love and brotherhood amongst all peoples, without bias, without hatred, without greed or jealousy!

Jewels of the Night

Jewels of the night
so glittering bright;
shattering the dark
are these city lights!

In places subdued
of every dark hue;
warding off fright
are these city lights!

Brightening the dreary,
comforting the weary,
making bold the leery
are these city lights!

They highlight the streets,
make cozy the homes,
and give bravado to old bones,
these city lights

Like diamonds in flight
when viewed from the heights,
they glow in the mist
on black eerie nights.

Ah, these city lights!

The Road to Nowhere

That long, long trail so lacking in care
Has branches scattered everywhere;
It empties off into a horizon bare,
That oft' traveled road to Nowhere!

Past mountains high and cities of glass,
palm trees tall and stone grass;
Scorched mercilessly by the unrelenting sun,
It seeks soothing coolness—of which there is none!

Through the desert's far reaches it runs.
To valleys wide and oases of sand,
Finding cactus, prairie dog, and towers of rock,
but not a drop of water—not one!

Far beyond vision, it trails on and on.
To what? We haven't a clue!
For those that travel it
returned not from the blue!

The Ordeal

I didn't sleep a wink all night. I tossed and turned as my tortured mind dredged up nightmarish images of the coming day; until finally, at dawn, exhausted, I dragged myself up with the rising sun, wishing I could be doing anything other than what I was about to do. A tiny but persistent voice nagged at me like a shrew, telling me I was crazy to be doing this and undermining my shaky confidence until the intervening hours became the longest, most dreadful ones of my life. I truly felt I would rather do most anything else than face this day. My mind procrastinated, but the body kept on tickin', as they say, and like a programmed robot, I went through the motions that were my daily routine. Arriving at my pre-appointed destination, all my savoir faire deserted me, burrowing into obscurity and leaving my mind as barren as Death Valley's desert floor. Though my demeanor seemed calm and self-assured, I was numb with fear!

It was all too soon that I was escorted into a room, stuffy with official, knowing faces that glowered as they hovered over me. Quivering like Jell-O and feeling claustrophobic, the voice of earlier began to taunt me once more. "Well, you've surely got yourself into a fine jar of pickles this time. It took real nerve coming here just like you'd fit in or something! What? Did you really think you could just walk in here and waltz your way through this? You don't know from nothing, girl! You presume you can match wits with these giants! Ha! Who do you think you're kidding anyway?" On and on it droned until its logic became impossible to ignore. This is for real, I thought, not just one of your super-duper daydreams. You're really here in this room … only this time, you won't wake up to find you've been dreaming again.

Scowling fiercely, the bearded wonder who'd been seated across from me finally left, and I heaved a muffled sigh of relief. He'd made me feel antsy, and I'm sure he was as unfavorably impressed with me; that is, if his lemon puss was any indication of his thoughts. By now, only one giant was left, and though he hadn't said much, he seemed relatively human. Well, at least he looked like he wouldn't bite! I assumed that his must be the decision process: yeah or nay. Oh, my God! He's going to read them again, I groaned to myself, as once more he began to shuffle through the paperwork I'd brought with me. What can he be looking for?

By this time, the smoke in the room was enough to make a freight train take a dirt road, and my lungs hurt from trying not to breathe it in. I really needed to get to some fresh air before my brain became addled for lack of oxygen. "Well," chirruped my cheery companion's voice—Oh, boy! Just what I didn't need!—"It was a game try." So convinced that I was doomed, it continued. "Maybe some other time and place where you're not so far in over your head, eh? Maybe you'll have better luck then!" All this negativity prompted a sudden need for a drink, a long, deep, and continuous one.

What? What was that he said? Had I heard him right? Do I *what?* Can I *what?* Exhilaration surged through my veins, and my heart thundered like a herd of stampeding steer across the plains. Was he really speaking to me in such positive terms about *my* future?

Chill! cautioned my ever-present mouthpiece of sage advice. Don't blow it now by blithering like an idiot. Play it cool, man. You expected this outcome and no other, right? Well then, let's have a little class here, huh? After all, you have got a few smarts! Don't you?

Who-o-o-p-p-e-e-e-e-e! I did it! *I got the job!* And here's hoping that's the last interview I'll ever have to sweat out again! *Whew!*

Western Wonder

Arizona's Western lands offer beauty rare,
Sun-warmed deserts and landscapes fair;
From the Phoenix Valley of Peoria and Mesa
To the red rock Stonehenges of Sedona.

There are incredible plants and colors so vivid,
The Francisco Mountain peaks that appear to be
Sprinkled with confectioners' sugar;
Beyond the yawning canyons of stunning grandeur
And the multi-hued glories of the Painted Desert floor.

These wearied plains of native lore,
Navajo, Hopi, Pima, Sinigua, and more,
Share sacred secrets from ancient times
Heard today … only as echoes through the pines.

No words can tell the true beauty of this land.
There are none to aptly describe it.
No photo, no matter how perfect, can do it proud.
It must be seen to be avowed!

This One Night

"I need you" are words
sometimes evoking more meaning
than saying the expected words—
"I love you"!

Tonight holds the promise that is ours alone.
For tomorrow, and all the tomorrows thereafter
will belong to her.

And I will be but a memory,
fading into the never-lands of yesterday,
while you will have each other.

Tonight—for just this one night—you belong to me!

There can be no tomorrows,
no happily ever after for you and I,
but you will be etched upon my life forever!

Because when I was alone and broken,
you were there ... giving selflessly,
filling the void, and asking nothing in return!

Anger: An Irrational Mind

Anger. It is powerful, unpredictable, sometimes raging and violent—and deadly! I use the sea for my visualization of volatile anger.

Though sometimes raging and violent, it can sometimes be deceptively calm and inviting without so much as a ripple to indicate the danger it holds. Its smooth glassy surface hides powerful undertows, churning ceaselessly deep beneath. It may appear tranquil, or it may be continually uproarious, lashing out unpredictably and in a seemingly spiteful manner. It has been known to rage out of control with deadly consequences, the kind only God can be the force to prevent.

This writing summarizes my irrational mind the night my life exploded into hellfire; its total consummate hatred unbridled, and the endless years to healing which eventually followed.

Had God allowed this all-consuming rage to prompt me to action, he would be in his grave today; and I would likely be on death row in some prison somewhere, if not already buried in some obscure grave, and only the Lord knows where my children would be. But for His Hand, I may have accomplished what I so irrationally determined to do—was driven to do!!!

I sat in the car and waited, numb all over; but when I saw him walking toward me, uncontrollable anger and hatred consumed me. Murderous rage, the red haze of an unbelievable, overwhelming, and completely evil desire to smash him into the brick wall he was now passing. It demanded ferociously that I stomp on the gas pedal and DO IT! Try as I might to obey this impulse, I could not move my foot to the pedal. It was frozen in place, though I willed it with all my might to move; and then he was there, climbing into the car, and the moment was lost!

Though the moment recedes, the anger remains, vehement as ever and ready to strike out at yet another time; but never again with such deadly rage, retreating instead into a glacial entombment of my own making!

As Time Has Gone

How much I once loved you;
how the ache still runs deep.
I hold your beloved face
within the dreams that I keep.

Your dark-eyed gaze
so steady, so warm;
the crevices of your smile
in the face of your newborn

A haunting memory;
an absolute love once shared.
This shredded heart of mine,
cannot be repaired.

Though years are gone, you are with me still.
The child I raised, I could not call Will;
but your smile he wears, my secret joy fulfilled.

His dark looks are the same,
even so, he cannot wear your name.

My Lisa, My Daughter

My Daughter ... What is she? Who is she to me?
What do I see when I look at her?
How does she make me feel when I think of her?

First, she is a child of God, of His Blessed Mother, and my child.
She is a person, a Very Special person!
She is a loving and caring woman of
Graciousness and beauty.

Her beauty is not just in her sweet, loving face,
But a real beauty that resides within.
She is naturally thoughtful of others, giving, and kind.
She is truly helpful, going out of her way to assist others in need,
Even strangers.

Unassuming, she does good as a part of her natural self.
She doesn't think twice about offering help;
Doing and giving simply because it needs to be done.
She doesn't hold grudges, is forgiving and loving,
Even when others are unlovable.

She is shyness and giggles and full of sweet thoughtful kindnesses.
She is blessed with clear skin, the color of peaches and roses; a
Copper gold mane and slate blue eyes. She has a soft button nose; coral
Pink lips and a pixie chin; and when she smiles, she makes my heart
Perk with joy!
More beautiful than the fairest of flowers; sweeter than the
Most aged of wines;
A beautiful darling daughter—and she is all mine!

I love you Lisa, with every bit of my capacity to love.

A New Home for Rose

The one we've loved has passed away,
Beyond our earthly sight.
She has left us and this world we know,
Without her warm, soft light.

But like a flickering candle flame,
Her light will always shine,
Brightening up another place,
More perfect, more divine!

And within the Holy Realm of Heaven,
She'll live forever more,
Warm and safe and bright,
In God's Eternal Light!

The Valley

A portrait of serenity is this beauteous terrain
on which still lingers a touch of God's name.
Amethystine mountains in the misty dawn,
verdant hills and golden meadows it spawns.

Brawny bronze oaks, majestic pine,
fiery maples blazing color divine:
Autumn's blush now drapes her in gold,
this jewel of the foothills, so clean from the mold.

Known as Schoharie, though not originally,
'tis the Valley of the Unforgotten Indian, you see.
They called her "Schohary," which in their tongue
means driftwood, a people just now being rightfully placed in
our history book.

For beauty rare, none can compare,
be it winter, summer, or spring;
each season brought forth is unique in its look,
inspirational to all made aware.

A lifetime of memories,
so exquisite *la faire,*
are forever embedded within.
For those so fortunate to have entered there,
But especially for those that remain therein.

CPSIA information can be obtained at www.ICGtesting.com
Printed in the USA
LVOW08s2315130314

377278LV00002B/3/P

Made in United States
Orlando, FL
09 May 2024

DATE: | |

My Beloved Husband...

DATE: | |

My Beloved Husband...

DATE: | |

My Beloved Husband...

DATE: | |

My Beloved Husband...

DATE: | |

My Beloved Husband...

DATE: | |

My Beloved Husband...

DATE: | |

My Beloved Husband...

DATE: / /

My Beloved Husband...

DATE: | |

My Beloved Husband...

DATE: | |

My Beloved Husband...

DATE: | |

My Beloved Husband...

DATE: | |

My Beloved Husband...

DATE: | |

My Beloved Husband...

DATE: | |

My Beloved Husband...

DATE: / /

My Beloved Husband...

DATE: | |

My Beloved Husband...

DATE: | |

My Beloved Husband...

DATE: | |

My Beloved Husband...

DATE: | |

My Beloved Husband...

DATE: | |

My Beloved Husband...

DATE: | |

My Beloved Husband...

DATE: | |

My Beloved Husband...

DATE: | |

My Beloved Husband...

DATE: / /

My Beloved Husband...

DATE: | |

My Beloved Husband...

DATE: / /

My Beloved Husband...

DATE: | |

My Beloved Husband...

DATE: | |

My Beloved Husband...

DATE: | |

My Beloved Husband...

DATE: | |

My Beloved Husband...

DATE: | |

My Beloved Husband...

DATE: / /

My Beloved Husband...

DATE: | |

My Beloved Husband...

DATE: | |

My Beloved Husband...

DATE: | |

My Beloved Husband...

DATE: | |

My Beloved Husband...

DATE: | |

My Beloved Husband...

DATE: | |

My Beloved Husband...

DATE: | |

My Beloved Husband...

DATE: | |

My Beloved Husband...

DATE: | |

My Beloved Husband...

DATE: | |

My Beloved Husband...

DATE: | |

My Beloved Husband...

DATE: | |

My Beloved Husband...

DATE: | |

My Beloved Husband...

DATE: | |

My Beloved Husband...

DATE: | |

My Beloved Husband...

DATE: / /

My Beloved Husband...

DATE: | |

My Beloved Husband...

DATE: | |

My Beloved Husband...

DATE: | |

My Beloved Husband...

DATE: | |

My Beloved Husband...

DATE: | |

My Beloved Husband...

DATE: | |

My Beloved Husband...

DATE: | |

My Beloved Husband...

DATE: | |

My Beloved Husband...

DATE: | |

My Beloved Husband...

DATE: | |

My Beloved Husband...

DATE: | |

My Beloved Husband...

DATE: | |

My Beloved Husband...

DATE: | |

My Beloved Husband...

DATE: | |

My Beloved Husband...

DATE: | |

My Beloved Husband...

DATE: | |

My Beloved Husband...

DATE: | |

My Beloved Husband...

DATE: | |

My Beloved Husband...

DATE: | |

My Beloved Husband...

DATE: | |

My Beloved Husband...

DATE: | |

My Beloved Husband...

DATE: / /

My Beloved Husband...

DATE: | |

My Beloved Husband...

DATE: | |

My Beloved Husband...

DATE: | |

My Beloved Husband...

DATE: | |

My Beloved Husband...

DATE: | |

My Beloved Husband...

DATE: | |

My Beloved Husband...

DATE: | |

My Beloved Husband...

DATE: | |

My Beloved Husband...

DATE: | |

My Beloved Husband...

DATE: | |

My Beloved Husband...

DATE: / /

My Beloved Husband...

DATE: | |

My Beloved Husband...

DATE: | |

My Beloved Husband...

DATE: | |

My Beloved Husband...

DATE: | |

My Beloved Husband...

DATE: / /

My Beloved Husband...

DATE: | |

My Beloved Husband...

DATE: | |

My Beloved Husband...

DATE: | |

My Beloved Husband...

DATE: | |

My Beloved Husband...

DATE: | |

My Beloved Husband...

DATE: | |

My Beloved Husband...

DATE: | |

My Beloved Husband...

DATE: | |

My Beloved Husband...

DATE: | |

My Beloved Husband...

DATE: | |

My Beloved Husband...

DATE: / /

My Beloved Husband...

DATE: | |

My Beloved Husband...

DATE: | |

My Beloved Husband...

DATE: | |

My Beloved Husband...

DATE: | |

My Beloved Husband...

DATE: | |

My Beloved Husband...

DATE: | |

My Beloved Husband...

DATE: | |

My Beloved Husband...

DATE: | |

My Beloved Husband...

DATE: | |

My Beloved Husband...

DATE: | |

My Beloved Husband...

DATE: | |

My Beloved Husband...

DATE: | |

My Beloved Husband...

This book belongs to: